BOOST YOUR SELF-CONFIDENCE:

A 21-DAY CHALLENGE TO HELP YOU ACHIEVE YOUR GOALS AND LIVE WELL

JUSTIN ALBERT

Copyright © 2014 by Justin Albert

WHY YOU SHOULD READ THIS BOOK

This book will help you renew your self-confidence and achieve your potential. It understands the stressors of your past and your present. Memories of your past force you to doubt your sense of self and your abilities in the crowded world around you. You are unable to formulate your own opinions, and you are unable to make new friends. This book's 21-Day Self-Confidence Challenge prescribes a single thing to focus on every day for 21 days. As you focus on your interior life, your exterior life will begin to bubble with positivity. As you renew your mind's strength, you'll see the world with a fresh zeal. You'll want to burst forth, achieve your goals, and reach self-fulfillment. Allow this book to help you take the first steps to rid yourself of past traumas and truly live in the moment.

TABLE OF CONTENTS

CHAPTER 1. SELF-CONFIDENCE: A JUMPING OFF POINT FOR THE REST OF YOUR LIFE

Self-confidence is the most important attribute you can have. It gives you the affirmation to move forward, to reach toward your goals and attain self-actualization. Your potential employers and teachers hope to work with self-confident individuals in order to maintain production in tight schedules. They aspire to work with someone who believes in a wholesome, complete product. All parents hope to create children with complete self-confidence in order to allow them an extra boost in the work and education culture. With self-confidence, you can find yourself living fluidly with friends by your side, with employers speaking to you like an equal rather than an employee. You can operate with new ideas, are unafraid of the future, and accept yourself the way you are.

WHAT IS SELF CONFIDENCE?

Self-confidence is an over-arching attitude. It is a feeling about yourself that allows you to hold ultimate positivity with an assured sense of reality. In other words: it allows you to see the very best of every situation in the proper context. For example, you trust your own abilities and feel in control of your life—to a point. You understand that you cannot do everything; your abilities limit you from certain actions. You may have the ability to play basketball because you have excellent reflexes, have an appropriate height, and can dribble between your legs. These are your abilities. However, these abilities do not transfer to other realms. For example, just because you can dribble between your legs and have incredible height doesn't mean you'll have the ability to swim a mile in a pool. Your abilities transfer only to specific areas of your life, and, if you have self-confidence, you understand the reality of that.

However, your lack of ability in one area does not affect your overall "mission" in the world. You understand your purpose, your goals, and you have the abilities to reach them. You expect to feel respect from your peers for your abilities and goals, and you therefore lend your own respect to your peers for their goals. Furthermore, you maintain a sense of humor. You don't feel the weight of the world; rather, you attain your goals without the undue stress that afflicts the majority of people. Even with your lack of stress, you are hardworking and dependable. You don't have negative stress pushing you to succeed; you simply have a drive to succeed for yourself, for the betterment of your personal goals.

WHEN DO YOU HONE YOUR SELF-CONFIDENCE?

Your self-confidence, or general self-esteem, stems from your very early development: your childhood experiences and the ways you remember them. You'll understand the ways in which these childhood experiences create poor self-confidence in the next chapter. Fortunately, you can drive forward from these past experiences to formulate new ideas of self-confidence, of self-worth. In order to fuel new self-confidence, you must adopt new behaviors. These behaviors must affirm your belief in yourself; they must be action-oriented, ready to charge signals to your brain that you have worth, that you have value. Self-confidence is all about assuring your interior self that your exterior self has value.

CREATING A BOND BETWEEN ACTION AND BELIEF

Your current perception of yourself is your belief-structure. Therefore, if you believe that you're not strong, if you maintain that you're incapable, you lack self-confidence and will therefore find no reason to meet your goals or succeed in your life. Fortunately, your actions can actually alter your beliefs. If you act like someone who is self-confident; if you radiate self-confidence through all you do and say, your actions will begin to feed your perception of yourself. You can alter your interior belief-system and begin to feel like a self-confident person on the inside. This will allow you to reach toward your goals, toward a more zealous sense of self.

Look to the behaviors of a self-confident person and begin to match what they do. Even if your interior self is a little "off" and lacking in self-confidence, you can begin to carry a different posture, a different manner. When your manner aligns with that of a self-confident person, you can feed a better interior sense of self.

6 BEHAVIORS RADIATING IN A SELF-CONFIDENT PERSON

Look for self-confident people in your life and try to understand them a little bit better. They are not naturally self-confident and happy every single day. Everyone has bad days, just like you. However, they understand how to alter their unhappy, not-so-confident days in order to fuel themselves through their actions with sure energy. As you speak with them and monitor their behaviors, try to find all seven of these behaviors in their actions and words.

1. *THEY ARE WILLING TO ACCEPT COMPLIMENTS.*

    When was the last time you didn't sidestep a compliment? Usually, a compliment leaves you spiraling out of control, refuting it. These self-confident people hear expressions of interest, of honor from their peers, and they don't refute them. Instead, they are gracious and accepting. They understand the joys of giving, and they allow their peers to receive that joy of giving by accepting the gift of a compliment. The self-confident people show complete appreciation.

2. *THEY RETAIN POSITIVITY IN EVERY CONVERSATION.*

    How often do you slide from initial greetings to complaints about what you have to do later, how much of a drag your life is right now, or how crappy the weather is? Self-confident people do not slide from positivity. Instead, they discuss their lives with joy and engagement while asking positive-oriented questions of their conversation partner.

3. *THEY VIEW LIMITLESS POTENTIAL AND*

OPPORTUNITY.

How often do you view a life-setback as an opportunity? Probably never. It's difficult to see beyond the initial failure to a new opportunity. Self-confident people, on the other hand, ratchet forward from this initial setback with positivity and a sense of optimism. They view this initial failure as a clean slate, a perfect jumping-off point. They don't allow the failure to rattle their sense of self.

4. *THEY FALL AWAY FROM SELF-PROMOTION.*

Do you find yourself bragging in order to feel approval from others? Self-confident people don't feel the need to shout out their accomplishments. They hold complete modesty and do not feel the intense desire to bring attention to themselves. If you find yourself bragging often, you probably feel that you don't deserve respect without calling out for it.

5. *THEY PROJECT INTERNAL CONFIDENCE.*

You recognize a self-confident person when you meet him on the street. He greets you with eye contact and a modest smile. His posture is tall, his gestures are confident. His body language is screaming his self-confidence. How do you talk and walk? Do you walk slowly, slouching? Do you greet people with a smile or a frown? Everything you do either translates your self-confidence or lack of esteem.

6. *THEY ACT AGAINST THEIR DOUBTS WITH POSITIVE ACTION.*

Above, you learned about aligning your beliefs with your actions. Self-confident people do not linger on beliefs that fuel them with doubt. Instead, they take action and boost their production, thus affirming any beliefs that they can do whatever it was they were a bit doubtful about. They busy their minds with solutions rather than their beliefs in the problems.

Chapter 2. Lack of Self-Confidence: Why It's Not Your Fault

Low self-confidence and lack of self-respect can stem from many places. Because this low self-confidence becomes simply a part of you, it's sometimes difficult to see it as something independent of yourself. It was, at one time, simply something separate that assimilated into a better, happier you. This low self-confidence formulated itself in you at perhaps an early age, and your behavior began to affirm your belief that you were not good enough, that you didn't deserve respect from you peers.

10 Hidden Reasons for Your Low Self-Confidence

Understand the ways in which low self-confidence became the bubbling monster inside you, inhibiting you from your true aspirations and from fruitful human relationships. Of course, low self-confidence can stem from many, many personal events. These ten are generally inclusive. They are the most common reasons for adult low self-confidence today.

1. *You had an uninvolved parent or caregiver.*

    During your first years, you were particularly

susceptible to your parent or caregiver's thoughts. You were aware when you did something to please them or when you did something entirely displeasing, like making a mess of the kitchen. However, if your parent was preoccupied or uninvolved with you as a child, you felt no desire or need to push yourself to achieve. When you did achieve something, your parent or caregiver gave no praise or no notice. Therefore, your achievement became unimportant to you because it held no light in your parent's eye. This initial feeling that everything you do doesn't matter can leave your adult self with the feeling that you are not accountable and that no one cares about you. You can feel unrecognized, disrespected. Oftentimes, if you have these carryover feelings from your past, you apologize for everything you do, even if that thing is good.

2. *YOU HAD A DISAPPROVING PARENT OR CAREGIVER.*

Your first years were spent hearing that whatever you did wasn't good enough. The achievements you produced at school or in your personal life were always met with parent criticism. This excessive criticism leaves you feeling unconfident in your body; it leaves you with the shame of constant failure.

3. *YOU HAD PARENTS IN CONSTANT CONFLICT.*

If your parents often fought when you were a child, you may have absorbed the negative emotions of your household. Oftentimes, children feel overwhelmed, like they caused the conflict and the disturbance between their parents. If this

8

happened to you, you may carry the feeling of being tainted, like everything you touch, everything you involve yourself in becomes scarred.

4. *YOU WERE BULLIED AND YOU HAD OVER-SUPPORTIVE PARENTS.*

It seems bizarre to link a lack of self-confidence and over-supportive parents. However, if you were bullied in school and you were met with parents who tried to hide you from the terrors of the world, you may be unprepared to handle the greater world as an adult. You were unable to develop an outer layer of protection. Therefore, when you try to embark into the world, you feel ill-prepared. Furthermore, your feeling of lack of preparation is shameful to you, leaving you to retreat back to familiarity in your parent's home. You feel your parent's high opinion of you; however, you understand that you just don't fit in the exterior world. Therefore, you feel an interior conflict between these two viewpoints. You feel that you aren't good enough to face anything that you don't already understand.

5. *YOU WERE BULLIED AND YOU HAD UNSUPPORTIVE PARENTS.*

To counter bullying with over-supportive parents, if you were bullied and you had unsupportive parents, you are plagued with a lack of self-confidence. You felt unsafe outside of your home environment only to return to a home without support, without love. You felt hopeless in your everyday life, and you brought these feelings into your adult life. You sense predators in all the people you meet, and you tend to feel that anyone who befriends you is doing you a favor.

6. *YOU WERE BULLIED AND YOU HAD UNINVOLVED PARENTS.*

If you were bullied only to return to a home without attention, without notice of your exterior problems, you felt shortchanged. You felt unsafe in your exterior world and unnoticed in your home life. This formed ideas of isolation in you, leaving you to feel that no one wanted to listen to your problems. No one wanted to give you advice. Your isolation may linger with you in your adult life, leaving you unable to talk out your problems because you don't feel like they're important to other people.

7. *YOU WERE A VICTIM OF A CERTAIN TRAUMA.*

Drastic physical, emotional, or sexual abuse brings a deep sense of low self-confidence and lack of trust in your adult life. You were forced into a strange emotional or physical position as a child, and your adult self has difficulty trusting anyone else. You may blame yourself for your past trauma in order to try to understand the trauma better, in order to make it your own. You may view yourself as a shameful person, a person who deserved what you went through when you were younger. In your adult life, you may not feel worthy enough to reach toward your goals or have meaningful relationships with people.

8. *YOU WERE MET WITH ACADEMIC CHALLENGES WITHOUT PARENT SUPPORT.*

Your school days were filled with ultimate confusion. You slipped further and further behind in your studies and felt that no one stepped in to accommodate you, to assist you with your academic endeavors. Therefore, you grew up feeling stupid or "less than." As an adult, you doubt yourself and your abilities. You don't share your own opinions because you feel that they are somehow defective or undefined. You feel ultimate shame in your intelligence abilities.

9. *YOU WERE NEGATIVELY AFFECTED BY THE MEDIA.*

As a child, you felt you couldn't measure up against the images on magazines, on billboards. You were never as thin or as beautiful as those people. Unfortunately, those images were airbrushed, altered. The people displayed lacked realistic qualities. Unfortunately, this feeling of inadequacy meets you around every turn even in your adult life as the airbrushing epidemic worsens. Even if your ultimate lack of self-confidence stems from a different childhood dilemma, this feeling of inadequacy in the media strengthens your negative feelings.

10. *YOU WERE A PART OF A PARTICULAR BELIEF SYSTEM.*

Many belief systems peg you into a place of perpetual sin. As a child, you felt like you were continually doing wrong, that you never measured up. You felt eternal guilt and shame during worship, and this passed on to your everyday life. You continually feel disappointment at your inability to reach perfection.

These unfortunate circumstances lead to low self-confidence. However, these experiences do not monitor your entire life if you take immediate action. You can alter the sense of yourself that you currently hold. You can look at your history in a different context and understand that the fault was often not yours. You can understand that the people who affected your perception of the world as a young child had great, low self-confidence, just like you do now. You can rectify your current feelings in order to stop the cycle. You don't have to pass on the low self-confidence to your children, to your friends.

Everyone holds his own path to feel safe, to feel self-confidence in his everyday life. Your path to find joy and forgiveness for both yourself and your past is different than anyone else's. However, you must try as best as you can to rid yourself of your life discomfort in order to find infinite self-confidence and self-affirmation.

CHAPTER 3. TAKING A SELF-INVENTORY: UNDERSTANDING YOURSELF ON A MORE INTIMATE LEVEL

Your low self-confidence is forcing you away from your goals and your true desires in life. You understand that your past probably had a great deal to do with you current feeling, and you understand that you must begin to act more confident in order to change your beliefs in yourself. However, there's more to achieving complete interior success than all that.

In order to move forward from your current disdain for yourself, your current low self-esteem, you must create a self-inventory. You must treat yourself like a manager would treat his store, for example. A manager would take inventory in order to avoid excess and make room for new things in his supply. Currently, on a general level, you understand that you have far too much low self-esteem in your inventory. You need to clear it out to make room for interior growth. If you don't take self-inventory of yourself, you will carry the dead weight from your past along with you for the rest of your life. It will push you away from your goals; it will hurt your chances of success.

13

Furthermore, you need to create a better environment for yourself. Your current environment is one in which you feel a lack of self-confidence. Is this lack of self-confidence purely internal, or does it stem at all from a negative environment? A self inventory will allow you to assess your personal situation.

QUESTIONS TO TAKE SELF INVENTORY

Ask yourself the following questions in order to assess your life on a very personal level. Answer the questions with complete truth. Remember, you can only move forward to self-confidence with a good perception of your reality, without the bad things you've been carrying around with you, and in a good environment.

1. *DOES YOUR LIFE AFFECT OTHER, SURROUNDING PEOPLE IN A NEGATIVE OR POSITIVE WAY?*

   Do you find that your actions or words negatively affect other people? Do you find that your actions—even if they come from a very deep, resentful place of low self-confidence—hurt your friends or family? Alternately, do you find that your actions promote others around you? Do you find that you are often building other people up with your words? Do people feel inspiration from you?

2. *WHAT ARE YOUR MORNING, AFTERNOON, AND EVENING ROUTINES?*

   Think about your daily routine. Think about how you wake up in the morning, what you usually

14

have for breakfast, to whom you speak, how you get to work, and how you get home. Think about every action you make throughout the day and think about its direct result. Are you seeing the results you want out of your everyday life, or do you feel that your days are lacking something? Try to alter a few of your routines in order to produce different results. For example, if you feel like you're overweight, you could begin waking up a little bit early and going for a walk or a jog. Just this simple act of changing a bit of your routine could alter the rest of your day's actions.

3. *WHAT, DO YOU THINK, IS GOOD ABOUT YOU?*

So often you're told not to spout your own praises. This is both true and false. As mentioned in chapter one, you shouldn't spout your own praises in order to receive praise from other people. This shows a lack of belief in your own abilities. However, understanding what you're good at on a personal level is incredibly important. Ask yourself: what is good about you? What would you say are your best, most personal strengths? Do you find yourself motivated by beautiful things? Are you creative? Do you have a love of mathematics? If you understand what your strengths are, you can push yourself down these particular areas in order to achieve your utmost success. You can paint a better picture of the person you are right now, rather than the person you were in the past. If you don't understand your strengths and only know your weaknesses, you will give yourself no real room to grow.

4. *WHAT GIVES YOU STRENGTH OR MAKES YOU*

FEEL INSPIRED?

Think about your life. What in your life gives you the strength to get up every morning? What has helped you come as far as you've come? What, for example, inspired you to read this book and work for better self-confidence? When you understand that, you can begin to nourish your inspiration and become even stronger.

5. *WHOM DO YOU ADMIRE IN YOUR LIFE?*

    Thinking about whom you admire in your life allows you to understand the qualities he or she has and how, exactly, he or she utilizes those qualities. Now, think about how that person might think about you. What qualities would he or she say they admire in you? List them.

6. *WHEN AND WHERE DO YOU FEEL MOST TRULY YOURSELF?*

    It's important to know when you feel most like yourself. Think about the environment you're in when you feel that way, and try to replicate the scenarios. In order to feel completely self-confident, you'll want to feel like you're representing your very best self. Therefore, a knowledge of how to be your best self all the time is incredibly important. What kind of people are you around? Are they the sort of people that build you up or tear you down? Is the environment a place known to you or unknown?

7. *WHAT MAKES YOUR PEERS COME TO YOU? WHAT IS YOUR PARTICULAR GIFT THAT ATTRACTS THEM TO YOU?*

Think about yourself in the context of your peers. Everyone has something he's good at. Everyone is separate from everyone else in very specific ways. There's something that you have that is special, that brings people to you asking for assistance or advice. Think about it. Are you especially good at cooking? Are you a good writer? Do you have athletic skills? There's something that makes you completely you.

CREATE YOUR OWN SELF-PORTRAIT FROM THIS SELF-INVENTORY

Remember how you answered each question and begin to write down things you like about yourself. Next, write down things that make you different from everyone else. If you see the ways you are different from everyone else—in new and vibrant ways—you'll begin to understand your unique personality and your unique place in the world. Make a sort of scrapbook utilizing personal photos, magazine clippings of things you like to do, or pictures of people you admire. Look at the scrapbook anytime you want to take a self-inventory and imagine your very best self.

If you're having a bad day, pull out the self-inventory questions and remind yourself all the things you're good at and all the things people appreciate about you. You don't have to think negatively about a specific event that you couldn't control; you don't want something you could have controlled to have negative effects on your progress toward self-confidence. Therefore, when something bad happens, focus on all the positivity in your life. Bring your mind to a different realm of thought.

Update your self-inventory every few months. Alter your written notes about your best self and reassign pictures to your scrapbook. Because you're always changing and working toward a better self-confidence, a better feeling about yourself, your self-inventory will have changed. Watch your scrapbook change over a period of years and feel your confidence growing.

CHAPTER 4. DAYS 1-4 OF YOUR 21-DAY SELF-CONFIDENCE CHALLENGE: A STEP-BY-STEP PLAN TO GAIN SELF-CONFIDENCE AND FEEL EMPOWERED: A UTILIZATION OF NEURO-LINGUISTIC PROGRAMMING

Take just twenty-one days to renew yourself, to fuel yourself with self-confidence and a boost of self-esteem. Take twenty-one days to rev your engines and take off from the standstill in which you find yourself. You're battling back against your past: the past that forced you down this road of low self-confidence. You're battling back against your interior voice: the voice that tells you that you are invalid, that you can't do anything. You're grabbing your sense of worth and taking small steps, every single day, to feel a renewed sense of power.

During this chapter, you'll take just one element of Neuro-Linguistic Programming's technology every day in order to fuel yourself and prepare yourself for the remaining days of the 21-Day Program.

NEURO-LINGUISTIC PROGRAMMING AND SELF-CONFIDENCE

Neuro-Linguistic Programming is the science of success,

of excellence. It analyzes the top people in each field in order to prescribe how those people think, feel, and act. Its thought is that anyone can learn how to feel, think, and act like these people, thus reaching their own personal success heights.

Essentially, Neuro-Linguistic Programming provides a link between how you think your interior thoughts, how you communicate on both a verbal and non-verbal landscape, and how you behave or work through your emotions. Because you hold within you a wealth of neurology, you are constantly conveying interior thoughts with information from your environment. Because you are a communicative animal, you immediately bring that information to light utilizing linguistic sounds. You transfer perceptions and beliefs into words, into communication. The general, overall analysis of your growth into a human being with patterns, with both internal and external behaviors, describes your programming. Therefore, how you think illustrates the Neuro pathways; how you communicate illustrates the linguistic pathways; how you behave illustrates your interior programming. Neuro-Linguistic Programming believes that if you can outline how these different pathways connect, you can understand precisely how you operate in your exterior, social interactions. You can analyze how self-confident people operate their particular mechanisms, and you can learn to match their operations. When you match these self-confident people's mannerisms, you are practicing a core belief of Neuro-Linguistic Programming. You are modeling.

When you practice Neuro-Linguistic Programming

techniques, you'll begin to observe humans in an entirely different way. You'll see different linguistic and behavioral patterns that alert you to people's inherent self-confidence or lack thereof. Understanding the ways in which these people communicate, however, will allow you to communicate more fruitfully with them. As you begin to diagnose how these people communicate, you'll have the ability to turn the conversation where you want it to go. For example, if the conversation is lingering on the negative side, you'll have the ability to ease the conversation toward a more positive light. As mentioned in previous chapters, self-confident individuals thrive on positivity; positive words shed more light on these feelings, thus rejuvenating them on an interior level. Your actions speak to your beliefs and strengthen them.

SUBMODALITIES AND CHANGING THE MEANING OF THE PAST

Another unique concept of Neuro-Linguistic Programming is the idea of "mapping" or submodalities. You have a map of your reality that is completely unique. This is because the way you perceive the world is completely different than the ways other people perceive this same world. You are complex in that the things that happened to you as a child altered you and formed you into who you are today, and these same things did not happen in the same, particular way to other people. You stored everything that ever happened to you with the use of your five senses. When you bring the same pattern of senses back into your mind, you can actually relive the experience. You can see the same visual patterns and colors; you can hear the same music; you can feel the same texture or smell the same smell.

In order to alter your reality and push back against things in your past that are breaking you down and forming low self-confidence in your present life, you can actually adjust the memory of these senses. You can change the meaning of the past by bringing new ideas down your neural pathways. When you offer your brain a better way to remember a past event, your brain will grasp at it. This aligns well with the idea of evolution: an organism will evolve for the betterment of itself, just as your neural pathways will reorganize their memories for a better, more fruitful interior life. With enough practice, you can train your brain to remember only the made-up understanding of an event rather than the past, actual event. You need to drop a past feeling of something in order to rejuvenate yourself and fuel yourself into a new beginning. In turn, this reduces your interior senses of stress, therefore giving your neural pathways a much-needed break. Stress from your past lingering in your neural pathways does nothing for you on a personal level or on a molecular level. Your brain will be happy to let everything go.

NEURO-LINGUISTIC PROGRAMMING AND ANCHORING

Do you know the story of Pavlov's dogs? As researcher Pavlov went to feed his dogs, he noticed that his dogs already had spit and slime coming from their mouths in preparation for the meal they were about to ingest. Therefore, his dogs' digestive systems were anticipating the coming of food.

Pavlov was interested in this conditioned idea that the

dogs' interior digestive systems could begin to prepare for food without first eating. In order to explore this idea more readily, he began ringing a bell every time he gave the dogs their evening meal. The dogs began to associate the bell with the meal. After several days, Pavlov rang the bell but did not deliver the food. He saw, however, that the dogs were so conditioned to the bell ringing that their digestive systems had already begun to operate. Slobber was sliding from their mouths.

Anchoring is classical conditioning. When you anchor something, you associate one, completely different thing, with a specific experience. In Pavlov's dogs' case, they associated the ringing bell with the experience of eating and feeling nourished.

The utilization of anchoring in Neuro-Linguistic Programming is this: when you anchor an experience or a feeling with an item, you can bring the feeling or experience back to your mind readily when you have a physical representation of the anchor. You can utilize an anchor, for example, to make yourself feel how happy you were when you saw someone you hadn't seen for a very long time. You can squeeze your ear and think about how happy you were over and over. After a while, when you squeeze your ear, you'll feel that happiness once again without even trying. You can actually alter your current mood by traveling, via your anchor, to a different state of mind.

DAYS 1-4 OF YOUR 21-DAY SELF-CONFIDENCE CHALLENGE: A STEP-BY-STEP PLAN TO GAIN SELF-CONFIDENCE AND FEEL EMPOWERED

The days leading up to your 21-day Self-Confidence Challenge, you must prepare yourself to be in a good mental state. This mental state allows you to try your absolute best to assimilate into the routine you're attempting to instate. You are attempting to feel valid enough to meet new people, to reach toward your goals, and feel a sense of vitality.

Remember that going into this, you must set realistic expectations for yourself. At the end of this 21-day challenge, for example, you will still have negative thoughts. You will still exist in the same strain of your environment. Your parents will still criticize you; your job will still irritate you. However, after this program, the way you act and receive the information from your environment will be completely different. You will no longer feel low self-confidence moving forward. Instead, you'll handle each individual problem as a person with self-confidence. You'll see yourself as a valid part of society, worthy of everyone's respect.

You will not reach perfection. Perfection is completely unattainable. However, if you remember to utilize these 21 Days of Tips, your self-confidence will begin its blossom. Remember that this challenge is not a get-confident-quick scheme. Instead, it is a renewed way of life. You must re-dress the way you live, alter the way you think in order to maintain true change.

Day 1: Engage in a Powerful Visual Exercise

Your first day of the 21-Day challenge finds you re-evaluating your sense of your future self. The technique utilizes your most powerful sense: your visual sense. The exercise creates a different neural pathway and a different way to communicate your new neural understanding to yourself and to others. Therefore, it brings a connection between your neural and linguistic pathways, altering your ultimate behavior. It is a Neuro-Linguistic Programming technique at its finest.

Find yourself a quiet, semi-dark area. Make sure you're completely alone. Begin by assimilating yourself in a peaceful state. Inhale and exhale very slowly. Bring your heartbeat to a lull. Feel every part of your body.

When you feel peaceful, open your eyes and imagine a mirror sitting in front of you. Inside the mirror, you see yourself. However, that image is a little bit different. That image is a self-confident, successful you. Imagine the "you" in this context. Imagine how this person walks, talks, and behaves in your usual settings. Are these behaviors different than your usual behaviors?

Next, place yourself in the immediate shoes of this person in the mirror. Imagine yourself as this confident "other" self. Feel yourself walking and talking just like this confident person. When you feel this confidence churning inside of you, cross your middle and ring finger together and say a particular word. Say something like: "Strength," or "Confidence." The word can be anything. The word should align with this feeling of confidence, and it should pair with the cross of your fingers. Repeat this process several times. As outlined above, you are anchoring this feeling of confidence.

Throughout this first day, remind yourself of this trigger several times. Imagine yourself as this "new and confident" person by crossing your fingers and saying your code word. Do this in various, safe locations first. Try it at the grocery store before you talk to the cashier, or try it before you talk to your spouse. It's only your first day with your anchor, but you can strengthen it in the days to come.

Day 2: Anchor Confidence in a Song

Music is charged with infinite feeling. You probably have a song that pumps you up: a song that makes you feel like you're on top of the world. The music can be from any genre, in any language. This song is already a sort of anchor in your life in that it allows you to feel better than you normally feel. However, you must strengthen this anchor.

Examples of excellent confidence-boosting songs are:

1. Eye of the Tiger by Survivor
2. Stronger by Kanye West feat. Daft Punk
3. Sexy and I Know It by LMFAO
4. Levels by Avicii

5. Another One Bites the Dust by Queen
6. Lose Yourself by Eminem

For day 2's challenge, you must begin your day by listening to the confidence-boosting song of your choice. Note: if you don't have one of your own, you can choose one of the above for your pump-up anthem. As you prepare for the day, listen to the song and imagine yourself as a more confident individual. Listen to it twice. Listen to it three times.

Later, when you're at work, when you feel uneasy, or you begin to feel a lack of self-confidence, pop this song onto your portable music player. Feel the good vibes you held in the morning pulse through you as you listen to the song. Remember how you visualized yourself, and begin to feel like that confident person you pictured. As you move forward through this program, you can utilize this song to boost your strength in any moment. It will be your constant companion, pushing you to move to the next day's challenge.

DAY 3: TRANSFER YOUR LEAST FAVORITE MEMORY INTO A POSITIVE ENCOUNTER

Bad memories tend to haunt people and alter their futures. Your bad memories, for example, inhibit you from living to your full potential. You remember something terrible that happened last time you tried a particular thing, and now you are wary of trying that thing again. This forms into a negative cycle.

For example, let's say that the last time you met new people, you were unable to open up and create any sort of relationship. You were embarrassed. Therefore, in the wake of that incident, you are afraid to meet new people because you feel that you will look silly, will be unable to form relationships, and will generally experience displeasure with yourself. Ultimately, this pattern leaves you no room to meet any new people or grow in new environments.

In order to break this cycle, you must change how you think about your past memory. This is outlined with Neuro-Linguistic Programming. You can relive the exact event, just as it was, with all of your sensory memories intact. If you want to alter the memory, you can do this by altering your sense memory. Bring a different light to the scene; allow it to have a different scent. Picture the memory of you meeting new people and being unable to present yourself well in a different way. Picture yourself acting just as yourself, interacting with people who also felt bizarre. Imagine that the people who you tried to make a connection with were also lacking in self-confidence. Imagine that they didn't think you were strange or without value. You were simply people trying to learn the best ways to communicate without the proper tools.

Begin by visualizing the real memory. Remember it for everything it was. Then, send it far back, away from your vision. Close your eyes and watch the memory fall away from you like a boomerang. When it comes back, the memory is the new memory with the different meaning. The memory finds two people simply trying to create a conversation and learning from the meeting. You understand that you were meant to meet that person in order to step up and fuel your conversational skills.

Picture the original memory again and then swish it back to the "new" memory. Do this many times. After at least ten times of visualizing this memory running away from you, try to remember the event in your head. Your neural passageways have assimilated a new formation. You will begin to remember only the pleasant, educational event.

Day 4: Make Early-Morning, Daily Affirmations

On the morning of day four, wake a half hour before you normally do. Go to a cool, quiet place away from everyone else in your house. Close your eyes and focus on your breathing. Descend into a meditative state.

As you linger in the meditative state, feeling your entire body working as one, feeling your neural passageways communicating the stance of your body in its environment, begin telling yourself affirmations. Tell yourself:

1. You hold the power to greatness.
2. You are, and have always been, a self-confident person.

Repeat these mantras to yourself, and add any that are specific to this day. For example, if you have a big presentation at work, tell yourself you are well-prepared and confident enough for the task. Repeat these mantras until they become engrained in your brain, ready for activation on your way to work.

Note: Remember to continue listening to your pump-up song, meditating, and keeping track of your neural passageways in order to maintain all you've learned in your initial four days.

CHAPTER 5. DAYS 5-8 OF YOUR 21-DAY SELF-CONFIDENCE CHALLENGE: CONFIDENCE TO STRENGTHEN YOUR SOCIAL INTERACTIONS

Now that you understand some very personal techniques to hone your interior thoughts about yourself, you can move on to the greater environment. You can begin to work on your communication, bringing your internal thoughts to the exterior, relationship sphere.

Friendships can be tricky. At their core, they're essentially two separate worlds colliding together and deciding, despite all differences, they'd like to coincide with one another and learn more about the other. It seems crazy, especially with the self-doubt creeping at you around every corner. How can you improve your ability to create a social life, and how can you hold the confidence to maintain strong social interactions? The following four days will allow you to focus on these ideas.

When you succeed in creating human friendships, however, you'll learn that friendships are key boosts to your self-esteem in countless ways. They help you make better decisions by giving you key advice for your tricky choices; they walk alongside you and see things from your perspective. They cheer you on when you succeed, and they comfort you when you fail. You don't have to go it alone when you have good friends by your side. But how, exactly, do you form these initial, fruitful relationships?

DAY 5: STRIKE UP A CONVERSATION AND SPEAK SLOWLY

Remember, in order for people to take you seriously, you must illustrate your confident sense of self. Sure, you haven't gotten to day 21 yet; you haven't renewed your complete sense of self-confidence. However, you can fake it. And, as mentioned before, faking confidence renews your belief in yourself on an internal level. Every little thing adds up.

Strike up a conversation with someone you've hardly spoken to before. If you have to, play your pump-up song from a previous day to prepare you to stretch yourself. Speak slowly, illustrating your authority. A person with authority shows their sense of confidence, shows the fact that they are worthy to speak to. Don't overdo it; however, slowing your regular, quick voice a few notches will boost your assuredness while talking to this new person. This new person will perceive you as someone he should continue talking to.

DAY 6: SEEK SOMEONE WHO CAN EMPOWER YOU WITH KNOWLEDGE

Knowledge is power. You've heard it a million times. However, fueling yourself with knowledge is one of the quickest strategies to begin feeling those waves of self-confidence. When you understand a new concept or learn a new fact, you are immediately boosted into a different world. Your environment alters.

Of course, you can empower yourself with this knowledge via the Internet. However, receiving knowledge from someone you seek out is much better. Call an acquaintance on the phone—someone you know has knowledge about something you don't. Approach someone at lunch. Remember that his perspective on life is completely different than yours; therefore, your life-knowledge is completely different than his. Swap knowledge and give each other pieces of each other's worlds. The person you approach will love discussing the knowledge he already has; he'll love speaking about himself and his world. Because you sought him out, he'll have a deep interest in what you have to say, as well. Open your eyes to the possibilities of knowledge.

DAY 7: FIND AN EXERCISE BUDDY

Exercising fuels empowerment, and empowerment creates boundless self-confidence. Ask an exercise-affluent person to go for a run or a walk with you. You're including him in something he already enjoys: exercise. Ask his exercise advice and tell him—in an incredibly positive manner—that you're hoping to get better in shape. Other people feel the joy emanating off of you when you make a decision to better yourself. Simply including them on your exercise journey will form a bond between you.

DAY 8: ELIMINATE TOXIC FRIENDS FROM YOUR LIFE

This is a heavy one. As you further your journey toward self-fulfillment and self-confidence, you must analyze your environment and reconsider precisely where your low self-esteem is coming from. Oftentimes, people find themselves in toxic relationships with negative friends, with friends who work to only bring them down instead of build them up.

Therefore, for day 8, ask yourself who your true friends are. Go through your contact list on your cell phone and analyze each name and your past history. If you find a name that makes you feel a lack of self-confidence, you must immediately delete that name from your contact information. Deleting them doesn't mean that person is cut from your life forever. It simply means you're taking a conscious action to eliminate a toxic environment while you heal.

Chapter 6. Days 9-12 of Your 21-Day Self-Confidence Challenge: Confidence in Your Romantic Life

The first 8 days of the 21-Day Challenge found you focusing on your internal self, altering the way you think about your past, and learning how to approach new people to begin forming human-to-human interactions.

The following four days will lend you insight on how to become more present in your romantic relationships. Each day is dependent on your current status: if you're married or single.

If you're single, the following four days will give you the confidence to approach people you already feel romantic toward or, perhaps, simply people you meet at random in your everyday life. Even if these approaches lead to absolutely nowhere, it's time you begin making a commitment to yourself and understand that you are good enough, well enough to have a romantic relationship.

If you're married or in a relationship, your relationship may have serious problems due to your lack of self-confidence. Your past days may have found you leaning heavily on this relationship as an unfair source of acceptance. You may have brought your insecurities into the relationship, bringing ideas that you aren't good enough for anything outside the relationship. These feelings may translate into the relationship.

For example, if something negative happens at work or at school, you may expect your partner to see you differently, to actively see your value declining. After a while, you may begin to devalue your partner. You may begin to contaminate him or her in your eyes, telling yourself that you don't require a partner anyway.

You must begin to restore this very real human relationship that has the potential strength to work you through every rough day—to work you through your low self-confidence to a better future. Your romantic relationships have true value when you enlist your energy to give them power.

DAY 9: MEDITATE ABOUT A PAST OR CURRENT RELATIONSHIP

When you wake up in the morning, go to your quiet, meditative ground and ask yourself some personal questions.

If you're in a relationship, ask yourself: How have you allowed the current relationship you're in to falter and fizzle? Can you see actual instances in your mind that formed this negative blood between the two of you? Do you feel your voice of self-doubt and low self-esteem working inside of you, altering the way you feel about your relationship without merit?

If you're not currently in a relationship, ask yourself if

these negative, low self-confidence thoughts have killed past relationships or are altering your ability to meet anyone new.

You must acknowledge the actual reason behind your faltering relationships or lack of relationships on an interior level. Only when you acknowledge these low beliefs in yourself can you rid yourself of them. As outlined above in the Neuro-Linguistic Programming section, you must picture yourself as a happier, more communicative person in a committed relationship. Spin your current thoughts of yourself into this thought and feel the way that happy, committed person feels. This committed feeling is your ultimate goal.

DAY 10: MAKE CONTINUED EYE CONTACT

During day 10, you must focus on making continued eye contact when you are speaking with either your romantic partner or a potential partner. You must make yourself seem open and positive, ready to listen to anything that person has to say. Now that you understand that your lack of self-confidence is putting a gap between the two of you, you can "act" your way out of low self-esteem. Remember that your exterior actions alter your interior beliefs. Furthermore, if you act confident, your romantic partner will feel that you are up to the challenge of being in a romantic, committed relationship. You will seem sure of yourself and ready to take on a future with that person, regardless of either of your faults.

DAY 11: APPRECIATE THE VALUE OF TOUCH

Affection can go a long way. Just feeling a small touch on your hand, on your elbow can bring endorphins to your brain, thus annihilating signs of stress. Unfortunately, you cannot actually ask for a touch on this road to self-confidence. Instead, you must be the provider of this touch. You must be the action-oriented person in this scenario to illustrate your depth of self-confidence.

If you have a spouse or a partner, remember to keep this touch in mind. Your relationship may be on the rocks due to your low self-confidence and lack of ability to love yourself. If you feel that you're unworthy of love, you may have been curling away from your partner, skipping out on this one big category.

When you see your partner in the morning, touch them on the shoulder. Kiss them on the cheek or on the mouth. Let them know, through pure physical actions, that you appreciate their existence. They'll begin to return this gesture of touch, showing signs of appreciation as well.

If you don't have a partner, this "touch" concept is still inclusive. In Europe, when people meet one another, they give each other two kisses: one on each cheek. You don't need to go this far. However, next time you meet someone you might have feelings for, reach across and shake his hand. Do physical things like opening the door for him, taking his coat. You don't have to physically touch him to give him the idea that you're physically "there" for them. However, you must stop closing yourself off.

DAY 12: CLAIM AN OUTSIDE INTEREST

Boost Your Self-Confidence

On day 12, you should focus on something that is uniquely for yourself—something outside of your relationship or your potential relationship. This thing could be a hobby, an exercise routine, or anything that puts your mind in a different zone. If you begin to hone your life outside of your relationship, you will begin to feel that you have more to offer in your relationship life.

For example: if you take up basketball as a hobby outside of your relationship, you'll have interesting stories to tell your partner or potential partner about last night's game. You'll seem interesting and more vibrant in the relationship because you have an interesting exterior life. You are well-rounded and able to exist outside of the realms of your romantic interactions.

Therefore, on this day 12, take stock of your old hobbies or anything new you might want to try. Sign up for an exercise class, head over to the craft shop, or enroll in a painting course.

CHAPTER 7. DAYS 13-16 OF YOUR 21-DAY SELF-CONFIDENCE CHALLENGE: CONFIDENCE TO FIND SUCCESS AT WORK OR SCHOOL

Low self-confidence at work or school can leave you feeling anxious and unable to truly succeed. Although you made it there: to your desired university or your workplace after extensive interviews and applications, you suddenly feel as if you don't belong there.

Your school or your workplace is, on so many levels, your identity. You must reaffirm your self-confidence in these environments in order to take a true stance in your life. Your workplace is your livelihood; it is the source of many of your relationships and approximately forty hours of your week. Your school life is the stepping-stone to your livelihood. It is, furthermore, the source of your relationships and so much of your time. Therefore, in order to maximize your life, you must maximize your time spent at these places.

DAY 13: OUTLINE THE REASONS YOU'RE AT THIS WORK OR SCHOOL

When you wake up before work or school on day 13, assemble a list of the reasons you were chosen to attend this school or be an employee at this workplace. This list must be specific. For example, in order to attend this university, you achieved all A's in high school. In order to be hired as an employee at your company, you had to rock the interview process and graduate from a university. List your accomplishments and your skills— the skills people see in you at work or school every single day.

By listing your skills, you'll stray your mind from your current panic-stance at your work or school place. You'll reaffirm your work or school identity.

DAY 14: REMEMBER THAT NO ASSIGNMENT IS OVERLY THREATENING

On day 14, you must be proactive about your thinking. Look ahead on your calendar and see your next "scary" day at work or school. Maybe you have to give a certain presentation, write a long paper, or give a speech. The low self-confident person inside of you may be screaming at these future days with complete fear.

During this day 14, however, you must remember that your perception of the situation is almost 100% of your truth of the situation. Therefore, you must alter your perception of the coming dark day. Instead of thinking of the presentation as a scary, terrible thing, think of it instead as a day that you can demonstrate all the hard work you've been doing. Try to work through this thought with your Neuro-Linguistic Programming techniques. Remember your last presentation. Is it forcing you to look to the future presentation with fear? Try to remember the last, bad presentation as it was, and then flip it on its head. Remember it differently. Remember it, instead, as a learning experience. When you drop the bad memory of presentations or tests, you can move forward to the next ones with a renewed sense of self.

DAY 15: TRY TO MAINTAIN ACTIVITY ALL DAY

As a low self-confident individual, you may find yourself hurting your chances of success. You think you'll fail, and therefore, you decide to fail to rid yourself of disappointment. This is the idea of self-sabotage.

This self-sabotage idea translates into the work or school place often in the form of procrastination. Because you have fear of failure, you simply put things off until the last minute until you couldn't possibly submit a valid piece of work.

In order to boost your self-confidence, you must practice the art of continually doing something. Doing something or making something evokes positivity. Even if your result isn't precisely what it needs to be, you still have the work ethic behind it. If you work toward something, you will ultimately feel better than if you sat there, feeling fearful.

Therefore, on day 15, arrive at work and take only one break: for lunch. Work from morning till evening without giving your brain a single moment to think about self-doubt. You'll find yourself utilizing your time much better; you'll stop lingering on things you can't change.

DAY 16: ADD A CHALLENGE TO SOMETHING YOU'VE MASTERED

At work or school, you probably have something that you do very well without thinking about it. Sure: this particular activity makes you feel good when you do it. However, you cannot allow this activity to remain stagnant. For example, if you're really good at presentations, you might begin to slough off on them because you think they're a sure thing.

In order to build your self-confidence, you must be willing to accept new challenges. If you add new elements to your presentation game, for example, you'll find your self-confidence growing exponentially. Not only are you good at presentations; you're able to innovate your presentations and make them more complex. Your boss will be incredibly impressed.

Therefore, on day 16, analyze what you're good at and up your game a little bit. Don't leave anything stagnant.

CHAPTER 8. DAYS 17-20 OF YOUR 21-DAY SELF-CONFIDENCE CHALLENGE: CONFIDENCE TO DEEPEN YOUR GOAL ACHIEVEMENTS IN ALL LIFE AREAS

The past 16 days have brought you affirmation. You understand the deep, engrained reasons for your low self-confidence, and you're beginning to work through them on a personal level. You have your pump-up song ready for any time you're feeling down, and you understand the benefits of Neuro-Linguistic Programming to refute bad memories and formulate them into something you can utilize for growth.

The following four days allow you to reach toward your goals in different areas of your life. You can work toward being a healthier, happier individual.

DAY 17: DRESS YOURSELF WELL

When you look the part of a successful person, you'll feel more like a successful person. If you refuse to wash your hair or wear nice clothes, you'll feel like you don't care about yourself. You'll give a message to the world that you don't care what they think about you, either.

Therefore, on this day 17 morning before you leave your house, do something extra special to improve your look. Try a new hairstyle; wear a different tie. Spruce yourself up in a unique way. Any alteration gives assurance to the world that you do care about yourself, that you are looking for improvement. You'll further assure the world that you're unafraid of trying new things. This confidence will affirm your interior beliefs.

DAY 18: SET A SMALL, ACHIEVABLE GOAL FOR YOURSELF

If your overarching goals are incredibly large, they can feel overwhelming. For example, many people have a large goal to lose a humongous amount of weight. When they pledge their goal to lose this amount of weight, they soon feel pushed against a wall. They can't possibly lose that much weight at once; therefore, they soon give up on their goal and go back to bad habits.

On this day 18, set a small goal for yourself: something that aligns on the path to your greater goal. If you set small goals, you can break your big goal up into more manageable pieces. For example, if your goal is to lose forty pounds, set a small goal for yourself to have a salad for dinner and go for a walk immediately after. If you achieve this goal, you'll show yourself that every day counts on the way to your big goal. You'll show yourself the beginning of a possibility.

DAY 19: PAY CLOSE ATTENTION TO YOUR INTERIOR DIALOGUE

Your interior dialogue is the voice in your head, constantly talking to yourself. You may have a voice in your head that continually tells you that you're not good enough, that you can't possibly succeed.

In order to reach toward your goals, you must take charge of that interior dialogue. On day 19, trace your thoughts very carefully. Whenever you feel yourself thinking something negative about your future or past self, take out a notebook and write three things you like about yourself. Remember: you won't show anyone this list. These sentences aren't proclamations to the world. Instead, they are affirmations that allow you to beat back against the negative voice in your head. Always write three powerful, positive things for every negative thought. Soon, you'll find yourself reveling in positivity.

DAY 20: BEGIN PRACTICING THE SKILLS YOU REQUIRE TO ACHIEVE YOUR GOAL

When you understand the goals for which you reach, you must begin honing the knowledge you require to meet those goals. For example, if your goal is to go to graduate school after undergraduate school, you must begin amplifying your knowledge about your particular subject. After all, you're looking to charge forward with this knowledge and become a master of your field.

This "knowledge" applies to so many different disciplines and goals. If your goal is to lose weight, begin to educate yourself about caloric contents and the foods you must eat in order to lose weight. Understand how many calories you need to eat every day in order to maintain your weight, and learn what your deficit should be. Working toward any goal requires much research and organization. If you have the tools to proceed, you must begin backing up your actions with education.

CHAPTER 9. DAY 21 OF YOUR 21-DAY SELF-CONFIDENCE CHALLENGE: MOVING FORWARD

DAY 21: KEEP STRETCHING

The past 20 days have allowed you to build a firm ground of self-confidence. You now understand the ways your brain operates and how it reacts to certain situations. You understand how to negate some of those negative thoughts and gear them toward a more powerful positivity.

Remember day 18. You achieved a small goal on a greater path to an ultimate goal. Keep this day in mind as you move forward, and set small goals for yourself each day in order to build your self-confidence. Continue to stretch yourself, like day 16's assignment, and boost your skills. Do a little something every single day to push yourself. If you continue the work toward self-confidence, you'll actually earn the positive feelings you'll hold. You'll earn these feelings and therefore find no reasons to refute them. They are yours. They are payment for your days of hard work.

Moving forward, it's important to remember to always act like a positive, self-confident person. Even when your life begins to crumble around the edges, you can charge toward your goals and bypass fallbacks with these honed techniques.

Remember not to give up on yourself. Remember that even the most self-confident individuals have low-confidence days. However, if you remember your goals, if you remember your powerful positivity, you'll have the ability to change everything.

ABOUT THE AUTHOR

My mission with this is to be able to help inspire and change the world, one reader at a time.

I want to provide the most amazing life tools that anyone can apply into their lives. It doesn't matter whether you have hit rock bottom in your life or your life is amazing and you want to keep taking it to another level.

If you are like me, then you are probably looking to become the best version of yourself. You are likely not to settle for an okay life. You want to live an extraordinary life. Not only to be filled within but also to contribute to society.

FREE PREVIEW OF

MOTIVATION:

GETTING MOTIVATED, FEELING MOTIVATED, STAYING MOTIVATED

JUSTIN ALBERT

WHY YOU SHOULD READ THIS BOOK

Motivation provides ultimate life fulfillment. It is the driving force behind every profession, every physical action. It fuels the creation of towering skyscrapers, five-star restaurant, and stellar paintings—

And yet: why is motivation so difficult to attain and maintain? Another thing: why is it so difficult to get out of bed? When did life get so out of hand?

This book analyzes these questions on both a scientific and emotional level. It lends the proper tools to build motivation in the wake of utter difficulty.

Motivation is pumping in every blood vessel, through every neuron. Human ancestors struggling to survive in the wild were fueled with this instinct: this motivation to persevere. Present people still pulse with this very intrinsic motivation. However, present-day people—because their needs are generally met, their food is generally supplied—must work for their motivation. They must keep eyes open; they must create their own understanding of their goals. Their goal is no longer: survive. Their goal is to prosper.

Procrastination. Stress. The dog needs walking, the cat needs fed. The work piles up, and motivation for desires and interests is simply out of reach. This Motivation E-book teaches the art of catching desires and interests once again and persevering. It outlines the ways one can work through the blocks in your path and attain that promotion, achieve that great legacy. One must do this:

51

reach for real, vibrant goals in order to attain real destiny—to know self-actualization. Only with self-actualization can one feel a renewed sense of prosperity, a full sense of self.

CHAPTER 1. MOTIVATION: THE ONLY ROAD TO GREATNESS

Humankind's all-inclusive goal is, effectively, one thing: to survive. The survival concept lurks behind all things in a person's life: behind every kitchen product, behind every home improvement store. And yet, naturally, this survival has changed over the years. It has diminished from something broad, something that must meet required caloric values and required habitat-levels into something much more refined.

What is, then, man's essential, present-day goal? To simply live. And to live well. To live better than man has before. And this goal requires innovation; it requires a push against the limits surrounding each person's life. Without breadth of motivation, people would not leave their beds; they wouldn't work to find a better life. Without motivation, people would have nothing.

Motivation is the call to action. It is the thing that pushes one from one's bed to greet the world and squeeze every ounce of energy from it. It is the thing that forces one to take one's proper stance in the world.

Do you feel, today, that you have the depth of motivation to reach your goals, to push yourself to the top of your career and become a prime person—a person with both physical and mental strength? Do you have the will to survive and the motivation to make the most of that survival?

Understand motivation and the current factors blocking
you from your complete embrace of your goals.
Understand the ways in which you can become the best
version of yourself.

WHAT IS MOTIVATION?

Understanding the precise utilization of motivation is
essential in order to prescribe everyday life goals;
prescribing life goals via motivation allows for forward-
motion.

DEFINITION OF MOTIVATION

Motivation, essentially, is that which initiates and
maintains goal-driven mannerisms. It is an unseen force.
Biological, cognitive, and social effects alter motivation;
these forces mold it, form it into something that either
allows growth or stagnation.

Biological effects on motivation involve the various
mechanisms required at a very physical level. As
aforementioned, one has kitchen appliances that rev and
whir in order to maintain a very base biological motive:
to boost one's caloric intake for further survival. One
reaches for a glass of Coca Cola, essentially, out of
motivation to quench one's thirst. These motives are
incredibly basic and biological; the animals and plants of
the earth have similar biological motivations, as well. A
human simply has refined his reach to maintain these
motivations.

Cognitive effects on motivation are incredibly
complicated. Hormonal imbalances, the things one eats
and the things by which one is surrounded can affect the

brain, thus altering one's motivational output. Depression, stress, and low self-esteems accumulate at this cognitive level and impair judgment, thus altering continued rev for motivation.

Social effects on motivation generally involve one's environment and cultural influence. What is expected of one in one's culture generally contributes to one's sense of motivation; for example, history finds women generally staying home with children. Their motivation could not grow due to social influences. Furthermore, one's parents and one's friends alter social motivation. If one lives in a stagnant environment—an environment featuring people without conscious effort, without conscious forward-motion, one might simply assimilate into this way of life. However, if one's parents expect certain successes, social motivation might be the factor contributing to one's college graduation, for example.

THREE COMPONENTS OF MOTIVATION

1) Activation
2) Persistence
3) Intensity

Activation is the primary component: the decision to begin. A person must make this conscious decision; it is the root of all motivation. It is the very thing that allows mature motivation to grow. For example, actively enrolling in an exercise class activates the motivation to become healthy and lose weight, thus improving one's life.

Persistence is the continuation of this activation. It involves one's push through obstacles after the initial activation. It involves intense, psychological strength. For example, after one enrolls in the exercise class with the obvious intention of becoming healthy and thin, persistence must step in to truly fuel motivation. After the exercise class begins, one must invest endless hours, limitless concentration, and physicality to the point of exhaustion. It is increasingly difficult to maintain the intensity. However, if one is fueled with the proper motivation, working through the exercise class until completion garners significant strength and benefits.

Finally, intensity measures one's level of vigor after initially activating and persisting. If one persists through the various exercise classes, for example, without a significant level of concentration and exertion, one is not truly motivated. One can persist, certainly. But one will not reach the final goal of true health and strength without full-throttle intensity. Find another example in university-level classes. One can activate one's enrollment; one can attend every class; but if one does not fuel every day with study and push one's self outside of class, one will probably not achieve maximum success.

EXTRINSIC MOTIVATION VERSUS INTRINSIC MOTIVATION

Motivation is found both extrinsically and intrinsically.

Extrinsic motivation exists outside the individual. Usually, it involves the motivation to pursue exterior rewards or trophies—things resulting from successes involving other people. Therefore, extrinsic motivation involves motivation from peers; it involves impressing others via one's success. One's competitive desire can drive this extrinsic motivation completely.

Intrinsic motivation, on the other hand, exists internally. The internal gratification of completing a very personal project, for example, fuels this intrinsic motivation. Perhaps one wants to finish cleaning and decorating one's bedroom simply to feel the fresh, open understanding that one's habitat is for one's self; one's habitat reflects one's life, after all. However, if one simply wants to decorate one's room in order to impress another person, this could deem extrinsic motivation. Essentially, if one is the sole operator of one's motivation without exterior benefit, one is fueled with intrinsic motivation.

A LIFE WITHOUT MOTIVATION: WHAT HAPPENS?

What happens without that pulsing drive of motivation? Where does this lack of motivation lead? Remember that motivation is the building block for all survival, all strength in existence. Furthermore, it is the real push behind desire and interest. It is the very thing that fuels the beautiful paintings in museums, the towering skyscrapers, and the countless football games. It is human's driving force toward the meaning of life.

FEELINGS OF FAILURE AND INADEQUACY

Without motivation, one cannot move forward with one's life. One must remain stagnant. Essentially, one's hometown becomes one's only town. One's first job becomes one's only job. Lack of motivation leads nowhere.

But this lack of push does not lead to a lack of feeling. Emotion is always at play. In fact, emotion is generally the pulse behind lack of motivation. These emotions come in forms like fear of failure, fear of the unknown, incredible stresses, and low self-esteem. If one cannot work through these emotions, one cannot build a solid motivational ground. And without this ground and garnered goals, failure and inadequacy sweep into the emotional mix. One can feel a loss: like the past few years of one's life went toward nothing. One can feel a desire to do it all over again—with that drive of motivation at their backs. Unfortunately, lost years don't come back around. And inadequacy and feelings of failure linger.

Fortunately, these feelings of inadequacy can be the very reason to push toward motivation and reach toward something else. Proper use of feelings is always important. Work toward the promotion you haven't even dreamed about; wonder why you never thought to go to the gym. Understand that there's a whole world out there waiting for you. Claim it.

CHAPTER 2. THEORIES OF MOTIVATION

Psychologists' motivation analysis involves several theories. They analyze the precise reasons why one is fueled with motivation—and why one may have difficulty jumping on the motivation train.

DRIVE THEORY

Behaviorist Clark Hull created the drive reduction theory of motivation in the 1940s and 1950s. He was one of the first scientists to attempt to understand the broad depth of human motivation.

HOMEOSTASIS: BALANCE AND EQUILIBRIUM

Hull's theories attend to the facts of homeostasis. Homeostasis is the fact that one's body constantly works to achieve balance, equilibrium. For example, one's body finds a consistent, approximate temperature of 98.6 degrees Fahrenheit. When one dips below or above this number, one's body hustles to achieve balance once more.

Essentially, the "drive" of drive theory refers to the tension aroused by the imbalance or lack of homeostasis in one's body. In the temperature case, therefore, one's interior drive is the fact that one's temperature is out of whack. Further drives are hunger and thirst. These drives, or stimuli, force one's body into action to achieve balance in the form of a meal or a glass of water.

59

Therefore, Hull's drive theory acts on a sort of stimulus-response mechanism. His theory is rooted in biology and therefore takes no notice of interior, life goals. However, he does provide a decent understanding of the root of motivation.

INSTINCT THEORY

Psychologist William McDougall studied the instinct theory in relation to human motivation. His essential findings rooted the instinct theory as a way through life—a way that assured continuation of life via natural selection. Of course, the behaviors he studied were not limited to biological needs. He studied human instinct; and human instinct garners several shades of gray.

WHAT IS AN INSTINCT?

An instinct involves a tendency to behave in a specific manner without engaging in thought. The acts are spontaneous, occurring in a sort of matter of course after a particular occurrence.

Human instincts cover a broad range of occurrences rooted in both physiological and psychological needs. Physiological motivations, of course, meet hunger, thirst, and habitation needs. Psychological motivations, however, clasp something a bit more human; things like: humor, curiosity, cleanliness, fear, anger, shame, and love.

MASLOW'S HIERARCHY OF NEEDS

Abraham Maslow's humanistic theory of motivation analyzes all the basic human elements—from the simplistic biological needs to the self-actualization needs.

He breaks these needs into five stages with the idea that one's motivations can only escalate when one's needs are met at the immediate stages.

STAGE 1: PHYSIOLOGICAL NEEDS

As aforementioned, physiological needs consist of the basic, survival needs like water, food, and sleep. One must meet these physiological needs prior to building the motivation to move to the next step.

STAGE 2: SAFETY NEEDS

These safety needs involve providing one's self with proper health, income, and an actual "home."

STAGE 3: LOVE/BELONGING NEEDS

After one meets physiological needs and one has a place to live, a place in which to feel whole, one can begin to understand the benefits of social surroundings. These benefits can fall from familial ties, friendship, work groups—anything that forms a sort of relationship in which one can beat back against loneliness and find a place in society.

Stage 4: Self-Esteem Needs

One jumps to the self esteem needs stage in the convenient stage after one feels a sense of belonging.

Learning that one "fits" in a society is a great link in the chain. Self-esteem needs allow one the motivation to achieve in one's school or work and to build one's reputation. It allows one to take responsibility of other things or other people. This is essential in the hierarchy of needs: that one does not "need" anything anymore—one is motivated, instead, to help other people meet their needs. One is further motivated to meet one's wants.

Stage 5: Self-Actualization Needs

Self-actualization involves something a bit deeper than the self-esteem stage. The self-esteem stage requires one to achieve in society, to take charge of one's self and one's life. However, the self-actualization stage motivates one to find personal growth, it motivates one to feel fulfilled by one's career, one's relationships. It might not be enough, for example, for one to simply achieve at one's job. This stage might require one to feel as if one's commitment to one's job is also making the world a better place, for example. One might do some soul-searching in this stage to truly understand one's place in the world. One cannot commit to this true soul-searching, of course, without meeting the initial four stages of the hierarchy of needs. However, to truly find one's self and truly meet one's goals, one must exist at this top stage—with all other needs completed.

Keep reading...

MOTIVATION:

GETTING MOTIVATED, FEELING MOTIVATED, STAYING MOTIVATED

ONE LAST THING...

If you enjoyed this book or found it useful I'd be very grateful if you'd post a short review on Amazon. Your support really does make a difference and I read all the reviews personally so I can get your feedback and make this book even better.

Thanks again for your support!

43174202R00040

Made in the USA
Charleston, SC
17 June 2015